The Legacy of Bill Russell

A Legend and A Champion Whose Impact Extends Far Beyond Boston Sports.

Mercy George

TABLE OF CONTENTS

PREAMBLE

CHAPTER ONE

RUSSELL WAS REGARDED FOR HIS PROMINENCE IN CIVIL RIGHTS ISSUES

CHAPTER TWO

RACIAL SCARS AND A MISSING MOTHER

CHAPTER THREE

HE SIGNED UP WITH THE CELTICS

CHAPTER FOUR

A DIFFERENT VIEW OF BOSTON

CHAPTER FIVE

HIS MARRIAGE

CHAPTER SIX

HIS ACCOMPLISHMENTS

CHAPTER SEVEN

WHAT CAUSED BILL RUSSELL'S DEATH, AND WHY?

CHAPTER EIGHT

A LOOK AT THE ORGANIZATION: BOSTON CELTICS

<u>CHAPTER NINE</u>

TOP 5 COACHES IN BOSTON CELTICS HISTORY

PREAMBLE

Bill Russell passed away on Sunday 31st July 2022. His defensive athleticism at center transformed the landscape of professional basketball and helped the Boston Celtics win 11 N.B.A. titles, the last two of which came after he was named the first Black head coach of a major American sports league. He was 88.

Red Auerbach, who engineered Russell's entrance as a Celtic and coached him on nine championship teams, referred to him as the single most devastating force in the history of the game when he was chosen for the Basketball Hall of Fame in 1975.

In a 1980 poll of basketball writers, conducted before Michael Jordan and LeBron James reached the scene, Russell was chosen as the greatest player in NBA history, and he was not the only one to hold that opinion.

The center position, historically a place for slow and bulky individuals, was altered by Russell's agility and his amazing ability to block shots. His incredible rebound set off a Celtic fast break that outran the whole of the NBA.

Russell was regarded as the brightest player to ever play the game and the model of a team leader by former senator Bill Bradley, who faced Russell when playing for the Knicks in the 1960s.

At his heart, Russell was aware that he stood out from other players because he was an innovator and that winning the game was essential to his identity. For The New York

Times, Bradley reviewed Russell's recollections of Auerbach in Red and Me: My Coach, My Lifelong Friend - 2009.

In the decades that followed Russell's retirement in 1969, when flashy plays delighted fans and team play was frequently an afterthought, his stature was further enhanced. He was remembered for his ability to highlight the skills of his teammates while controlling the action, and to do so without bravado: He detested dunking or gesturing to celebrate his feats.

In those later years, with his trademark white goatee, Russell made an appearance on the floor in the spring to present the 2009 Russell Trophy to the NBA Championship Series Most Valuable Player.

CHAPTER ONE

Russell Was Regarded for His Prominence in Civil Rights Issues

He participated in the 1963 March on Washington for Jobs and Freedom, and he watched the Rev. Dr. Martin Luther King Jr. deliver his I Have a Dream speech from the front row of the audience. After the assassination of civil rights pioneer Medgar Evers, he traveled to Mississippi and joined forces with Charles Evers, Medgar's brother, to launch an integrated basketball camp in Jackson. He was one of many well-known Black sports figures that supported Muhammad Ali after Ali decided against enlisting in the military during the Vietnam War.

At the White House in 2011, President Barack Obama presented Russell with the Presidential Medal of Freedom, the country's highest civilian honor, in recognition of his defense of the rights and dignity of all men.

Russell shared a picture of himself kneeling while holding the trophy on Twitter in September 2017 in response to President Donald J. Trump's call for NFL owners to fire players protesting racial injustice by kneeling during the national anthem.

I just wanted to let those guys know that I'm behind them, he said to ESPN.

At 6 feet 10 inches and 220 pounds, Russell was a reedy, towering figure. He was cagey under the hoop, able to anticipate an opponent's shoots and get into position for a rebound. Additionally, his amazing leaping skills made it nearly certain that he would catch the ball if it caromed off the hoop. His longtime nemesis Wilt Chamberlain, who had three inches on him, concluded his career as the No. 2 rebounder in NBA history.

Russell grabbed 21,620 rebounds, an incredible 22.5 per game on average, with a single-game high of 51 against the Syracuse Nationals, the team that would later become the Philadelphia 76ers in 1960.

He didn't have a great shooting touch, but he scored 14,522 points, or 15.1 a game, on average, including many high-percentage, short left-handed hook jumpers. Because such records were not kept in his day, the total number of his blocked shots is unknown, but they had an impact on games.

Russell may come off as distant outside of the court. Both the prevalent bigotry in Boston and the humiliations his family had through in segregated Louisiana when he was a child had left them scarred. He was the team's lone Black player when he signed with the Celtics in 1956. His Reading, Massachusetts, home was broken into in the early 1960s.

Not the city of Boston or the supporters, Russell's primary commitment was to his teammates. He refused to sign autographs for spectators or even for his colleagues as mementos since he valued his solitude and despised public demonstrations of admiration. In March 1972, the Celtics held a private ceremony in Boston Garden to retire his No. 6 at his request. He declined to attend the ceremony despite being elected to the Naismith Memorial Basketball Hall of Fame, which is in Springfield, Massachusetts, right in the heart of Celtics territory.

CHAPTER TWO

Racial Scars and a Missing Mother

At Monroe, Louisiana, where his father Charles worked in a paper bag mill, William Felton Russell was born on February 12th, 1934. Although his youth was scarred by racism, he remembers a pleasant home life.

He remembered a policeman once threatening to arrest his mother, Katie, because she was sporting a fashionable attire similar to those worn by white ladies. Bill was present when a petrol station employee attempted to humiliate his father by refusing to offer service. Charles Russell chased the employee while brandishing a tire iron, and the incident came to an end.

Bill's family moved to Oakland, California, when he was nine years old. When his mother passed away when he was 12 years old, his father, who had started a trucking company and then worked in a foundry, was left to raise Bill and his brother, Charles Jr., instilling in them the values of working hard, valuing self-worth, and independence, as Russell has long recalled.

Russell, who placed a strong emphasis on defense and rebounding, started as a senior for the basketball team at McClymonds High School in Oakland. Hal DeJulio, a former basketball player for the University of San Francisco who served as a scout for his alma university, saw Russell's potential and suggested that Phil Woolpert, the coach, hire him.

With the help of guard K.C. Jones, a future Celtic teammate, Russell led San Francisco to N.C.A.A. championships in each of his final two seasons after receiving a scholarship and going on to become an All-American. The squad won 55 straight games after suffering a setback against U.C.L.A. in Russell's junior season. In each of his three varsity seasons, he scored more than 20 points and grabbed more than 20 rebounds.

In 1963, Russell told Sport magazine about his time playing basketball in college: Nobody had ever played basketball the way I played it, or as well. They had never witnessed a shot blocker before. Now I will be arrogant: I like to think I invented a completely new genre of play.

Midway through the 1950s, the Celtics had a team with a lot of talent that included Ed Macauley, a brilliant shooter up front, Bill Sharman, the league's best guard, and Bob Cousy, the best small man in the league. But because they lacked a strong center, they had never claimed a championship.

The Rochester Royals held the No. 1 pick in the 1956 N.B.A. draft, but they already had a standout big man in Maurice Stokes, and their owner, Les Harrison, was unwilling to engage in what he thought would be a bidding war with the Harlem Globetrotters, who were reportedly willing to offer Russell a lucrative contract, for Russell. In response, the Royals selected Duquesne guard Sihugo Green.

The No. 2 draft pick went to the St. Louis Hawks, but they also did not believe they could afford Russell. In exchange for Macauley, a St. Louis native, and Cliff Hagan, a potential rookie, Auerbach persuaded them to transfer that pick to the Celtics. Boston was able to hire Russell as a result.

Russell did have a meeting with the Globetrotters that spring, but he claimed he had no serious interest in joining with them in a January 1958 article he co-wrote with Al Hirshberg for The Saturday Evening Post. He commented that he did not find the idea of traveling the world for an entire year intriguing and that since their area of expertise is clowning, he did not want to be known as a humorous man wearing a basketball uniform.

CHAPTER THREE

He Signed Up with the Celtics

After leading the American Olympic team to victory in the 1956 Melbourne Games, Russell signed up with the Celtics in December. He averaged 19.6 rebounds while participating in 48 games as a rookie.

That Celtic team, which included Frank Ramsey, Russell, Cousy, Sharman, high-scoring rookie Tom Heinsohn, and the powerful Jim Loscutoff, won the team's first NBA championship by defeating the Hawks in the championship game.

Enter Chamberlain Russell, who won his first MVP honor in his second season. However, this time, the Hawks defeated the Celtics to win the championship, dominating after

Russell suffered an ankle injury in Game 3 of the championship series. The Celtics began their run of eight straight titles the following year when they won the Championship again.

The 7-foot-1, 275-pound Chamberlain joined the Philadelphia Warriors in Russell's fourth season - 1959–60 - and made his NBA debut. As a rookie, Chamberlain led the league in scoring with 37.6 points per game and outperformed Russell in rebounding, averaging 27 per game to Russell's 24. However, the Celtics once again won the championship.

Russell was quick, and Chamberlain embodied strength and force. In their games, Chamberlain typically outscored Russell and grabbed more rebounds, but the Celtics won the majority of them.

Bill Russell and the Celtics, in Chamberlain's words, were a good match.

Russell, who was good friends with Chamberlain off the court, complimented him in return. I get that people make reference to me having more titles, but I fail to see how Wilt could be held accountable for that, he added. Everyone lost to us. Wilt wasn't the only one.

Russel and Chamberlain had a bitter rivalry. In Cousy on the Celtic Mystique - 1988, a book he co-wrote with Bob Ryan, Cousy recalled that Russell terrified him. Wilt may say anything he wants, but in the past, I've seen Wilt assert himself physically against everyone else but not Russell.

In order to force Chamberlain to modify the angle of his fadeaway jump jumpers and release them farther from the basket than he preferred, Russell used a close-quarters defense on him.

In another aspect, Russell triumphed over Chamberlain: He claimed that at his prime, his yearly income was $100,001, or $1 more than Chamberlain was earning.

Russell was a fierce competitor who, although claiming he wasn't anxious before games, had a ritual in the locker room that was frequently seen.

He admitted to The Boston Globe in 2009, I puked, but I was never ill. It served as a means for my body to eliminate all excesses.

It was a thunderous noise, almost as loud as his laugh, according to Celtics forward John Havlicek.

In December 1968, Havlicek stated to Sports Illustrated, He does not really frequently do it today, unless it is a vital game or a huge test for him - someone like Chamberlain, or someone coming up that everyone is hyping. We all smirked in the locker room and remarked, we are going to be OK tonight. Additionally, it sounds good and conveys his enthusiasm for the game.

Russell exuded dominance before the game even started. While the other players rushed onto the floor to make their entrances, Russell walked over, his goatee lending a threatening aura at a time when few players wore facial hair.

Russell remembered, that he would glare at everyone with contempt, like a lazy dragon who cannot be bothered to chase off another would-be hero. Hey, the king is here tonight, he wanted his appearance to be announced.

When he started blocking shots that would become obvious.

According to Red Auerbach: An Autobiography - 1977, which he co-wrote with Joe Fitzgerald, Russell turned shot-blocking into an art. We would be on the fast break as soon as he would pop the ball straight up and grab it like a rebound, or he would guide it directly into the path of one of his friends. Russell did not ever hit a ball into the third balcony as those other guys did.

Russell was not the first Black head coach in professional sports, but he had the biggest influence because he was the first person of color to be selected in 1966 to coach a team in one of the top sports leagues in the United States. Star running back Fritz Pollard once served as a coach in the National Football League, but that was back when the league was just getting started in the 1920s. In 1961–1962, John McLendon served as the head coach of the American Basketball League's Cleveland Pipers, but the A.B.A. was only a minor draw.

In Russell's first season as a coach, the Celtics' eight-year winning streak was broken, but it required one of the NBA's finest teams to accomplish it. The Philadelphia 76ers, who went 68-13 and had Chamberlain, Luke Jackson, Chet Walker,

Hal Greer, and Billy Cunningham in their roster, defeated the 1966–1967 Celtics in the Eastern Conference playoff finals despite having a better regular season record -60–21.

CHAPTER FOUR

A Different View of Boston

Auerbach found excellent replacements for the Celtic players from Russell's rookie season, most notably Havlicek at forward and Sam Jones and K.C. Jones, Russell's former college teammate, at guard.

In Russell's final two seasons as a player-coach for the Celtics, they won NBA championships. In the 1969 NBA Finals, he defeated a Laker squad that also included Jerry West, Elgin Baylor, and the newly acquired Wilt Chamberlain to win the championship.

When Russell was a player and Boston's de facto segregated schools were making national headlines, Russell could not easily forget the city.

Russell stated in Second Wind: To me, Boston itself was a flea market of racism. It contained all kinds in their most virulent state, both old and new. Long before they emerged in New York, the city had racists who were corrupt, city-hall cronies, brick-throwing, send-them-back-to-Africa racists, and in the university neighborhoods, false radical-chic racists.

But the city evolved over time, and so did his impression of it.

In the weeks before the 2004 Democratic National Convention, which was held in Boston, Russell contributed to its promotion with a radio ad. I believe a lot of things are taking place to make it a welcoming city where everyone is accepted and no one is excluded, he remarked.

In 2013, Boston dedicated a bronze statue commemorating Russell in City Hall Plaza.

In his later years, Cousy felt guilt for not speaking out against the racism Russell experienced while they were teammates, and in February 2016, he wrote Russell a letter of apology.

Russell did not contact Cousy until after two and a half years had gone, according to Gary M. Pomerantz's account in his book The Last Pass: Cousy, Russell, the Celtics, and What Matters in the End - 2018. Russell then called him.

Cousy enquired as to whether Russell had got the letter.

Pomerantz reported that Russ had claimed he had. About it, nothing more was said. Cooz had hoped that their discussion would progress to a more important topic. Even yet, he had given Russ one last pass. He was content.

In the early 1970s, Russell worked as an ABC Sports commentator for N.B.A. games. His elevated chuckling laugh on the air revealed a side of him to audiences that only his colleagues had seen. He then resumed coaching.

In 1973, he was appointed coach and general manager of the Seattle SuperSonics, taking over a franchise that had not reached the playoffs in its previous six seasons. In his four seasons in that position, he guided the team to two playoff appearances.

When the Sacramento Kings were mired in a 17-41 record in March 1988, he was fired as coach and given the vice president position in charge of basketball operations. In December 1989, he was let go from that position.

Russell remained approachable and took advantage of business chances well after his NBA career was over.

In 1999, he consented to a public ceremony at the Fleet Center, which replaced Boston Garden, to commemorate his previous championship team's 30th anniversary, his retirement as a player, and the second retirement of his jersey number. The National Mentoring Partnership, whose programs he had helped create as a board member, was also raising money during the event.

In this nation, he informed the audience, there are no other people's children. They are the nation's future, and he would not wage war on them. He will always do what he can to improve a child's life.

In addition to doing commercials and giving motivational talks, he also signed autographs for serious collectors for a price.

CHAPTER FIVE

His Marriage

In 2016, Russell tied the knot with Jeannine Fiorito for the fourth time. Both his first and second marriages—to Rose Swisher and Dorothy Anstett—ended in divorce. He lost his third wife, Marilyn Nault, in 2009 at the age of 59.

William Jr., Jacob, and Karen Kenyatta Russell, his three children from his first marriage, were born to Russell. At the age of 58, Buddha, aka William Jr., passed away in 2016. Russell's brother Charlie L. Russell, a playwright and screenwriter, passed away in 2013 at the age of 81.

When it came to his beliefs, Russell did not give in. He told Sport magazine in 1963 that there are two societies in this country, and he said he had to acknowledge this in order to view life for what it was and avoid going stark, raving insane. I do not strive for approval. It is who I am. That is great if you like it. If not, I could not give a damn.

In 1999, he told Sports Illustrated that it does become art if you can elevate it to a height that only a select few of individuals can.

CHAPTER SIX

His Accomplishments

Bill Russell, who passed away at the age of 88, was a multi-talented athlete who excelled at basketball. In addition to his work in professional athletics, Russell was a devoted advocate for human rights.

He was a 12-time NBA All-Star as well as the NBA MVP five times. In 1955 and 1956, he also guided the San Francisco Dons to back-to-back NCAA titles. In addition, he led the American basketball team to a gold medal at the 1956 Summer Olympics.

In the East Room of the White House in February 2011, Barack Obama gave Russell the Presidential Medal of Freedom. He discussed Russell's record of winning 11 NBA championships—more than any other player in history. While representing the Boston Celtics, all titles were won.

The president was more struck by Russell's life than by his athletic prowess, noting that he had marched with Martin Luther King Jr., supported Muhammad Ali, and boycotted a Kentucky game after his Black teammates were turned away from a coffee shop.

Obama stated in 2011 that despite being subjected to taunts and acts of vandalism, he persisted in his commitment to improving the play of his beloved teammates and paving the way for the success of countless others. And I hope that one day, kids in Boston's streets will gaze up at a statue honoring both Bill Russell the man and Bill Russell the athlete.

CHAPTER SEVEN

What Caused Bill Russell's Death, And Why?

His family announced Bill Russell's passing on Twitter. They did not, however, provide a precise cause of death. Russell was said to have passed away naturally from old age.

Russell was admitted to the hospital four years ago for dehydration but quickly made a full recovery. At that time, it was discovered that he also has some respiratory challenges and heart problems brought on by aging. These are thought to have been the final factor in his passing.

He was diagnosed with dehydration when he was hospitalized four years ago. He apparently has respiratory challenges as well as heart problems.

Both on and off the field, Bill Russell had a successful career.

Bill Russell was given the name William Felton Russell at birth on February 12th, 1934. He was an American basketball player who played center for the NBA's Boston Celtics. He guided the team to the championship a record 11 times throughout the course of his illustrious 13-year career.

Bill Russell is remembered by the NBA community.

Bill Russell, a deceased great, has been honored by NBA players, fans, and the general public. The guy who was instrumental in the transformation in American sports history has received innumerable tributes honoring his illustrious career.

In a statement, the Boston Celtics said: It seems unimaginable to be the greatest champion in your sport, to revolutionize how it is played, and to be a cultural leader all at once, but that is who Bill Russell was.

Every aspect of the Celtics organization bears traces of Bill Russell, from the organization's devotion to social justice and civil rights off the court to its unwavering pursuit of greatness and appreciation of team accomplishments above individual glory. His family is in our thoughts as we grieve his passing and honor his great contribution to basketball, Boston, and beyond.

An all-time great and additional NBA legend Bill Russell was a pioneer in many ways, including as a player, a champion, the NBA's first Black head coach, and an activist, according to Michael Jordan. For every Black player who entered the league after him, including myself, he paved the road and served as an example. A legend has left this planet.

As tall as Bill Russell was, the former president Barack Obama claimed that his legacy is much greater than that, both as a player and as a person. Russell was also hailed by President Biden as a titanic warrior for liberty, justice, and equality.

These are just a few of the compliments people have for Russell. He will always be cherished in this world. May God grant him eternal peace. His family has our sympathy during this trying time.

CHAPTER EIGHT

A Look at the Organization: Boston Celtics

A Boston, Massachusetts-based American basketball team. The Celtics, one of the most successful teams in sports history, won 11 of the National Basket Association championships between 1957 and 1969. They have amassed 17 NBA championships overall.

The Celtics, founded in Boston by Walter Brown in 1946, were founding members of the Basketball Association of America, a precursor to the NBA, which was founded in 1949. When the organization was first established, Brown also oversaw the Boston Garden, whose characteristic parquet court the green-and-white Celtics dominated until the team relocated to a new facility, now known as TD Garden, in 1995-96. Each of the team's first four seasons ended in defeat, which led to the 1950 appointment of Red Auerbach as head coach.

Midway through the 1950s, the Celtics were led by Auerbach, who eventually served as the team's president and general manager. After defeating the St. Louis Hawks in a hotly contested championship series that included a seventh game decided in double overtime during the 1956–57 season, the franchise won its first championship. The Celtics won eight straight NBA championships between 1958-59 and 1965-66, a record for the four major North American team sports, and won again in 1967-68 and 1968-69 with a lineup of Hall of Famers that included Frank Ramsey, Ed Macauley, Bill Sharman, ball-handling wizard Bob Cousy, Tom Heinsohn, and dominating center Bill Russell, who was named the league's MVP five times. They also had Sam Jones, K.C. Jones, and John Hay.

The growth of television in the US following World War II and Boston's rise coincided helped the team and its players become famous personalities as the sport's national reputation increased. Two instances of Russell collecting an NBA Finals-record 40 rebounds in a game—in 1960 and 1962—and Havlicek's series-clinching steal of an inbounds pass in game seven of the 1965 Eastern Division finals—which prompted broadcaster Johnny Most to yell, Havlicek stole the ball!—are among the standouts of the Celtics' historic championship run. The contests between Wilt Chamberlain and Russell, first as a Philadelphia 76er and then with the Los Angeles Lakers, were at the heart of some of the most thrilling games in NBA postseason history. Wilt Chamberlain functioned as the Celtics' player-coach from 1966 to 1969.

On the Heinsohn-coached teams that won championships in 1973–74 and 1975–76, Havlicek continued to play a significant role alongside Dave Cowens, Paul Silas, and Jo Jo White. For the second of those titles, game five of the finals featured a thrilling triple-overtime victory over the Phoenix Suns. After the NBA prevented the team's owner, Irv Levin, from relocating the club to his native California, the Celtics were involved in an unusual deal in 1978. Instead, John Y. Brown, the owner of the Buffalo Braves, and Levin exchanged franchises. When they selected sharpshooting forward Larry Bird in the NBA draft that same year, Boston made history by acquiring one of the best players in league history—and possibly the most adored Celtic of all time. The superiority conflict between the Lakers, led by Magic Johnson, and a Celtics team, led by Bird, Robert Parish, Kelvin McHale, and Dennis Johnson, that advanced to the NBA finals five times in the 1980s and won championships in 1980–81, 1983–84, and 1985–86, engendered enthusiasm that helped the NBA reach new heights of prominence.

Six years starting with the 1995–96 season marked the first extended postseason drought in the franchise's history for the Celtics during this time period. The Celtics frequently fell in the first round when they made a postseason comeback. This changed during the 2007–08 NBA season, when the Celtics underwent the single most significant change of direction in league history, completing with the league's best record and submitting a 42–win increase following the offseason addition of superstars Kelvin Garnett and Ray Allen to a team that already included a longstanding All-Star in Paul Pierce. They made it to the NBA finals where they overcame the rival Lakers once more to win their ninth championship overall. The two teams competed for the NBA championship in the 2009–10 season after winning their respective conference titles once more. The Lakers prevailed in the finals in seven games.

In the 19th century, English jails utilized treadmills as a form of punishment for inmates. Treadmills have been used in muscle-powered machines since ancient times.

The Celtics experienced less on-court success as their seasoned roster became older. In an effort to jumpstart a rebuilding phase centered on younger players, Allen left the team in free agency in 2012, while the franchise traded away Garnett and Pierce after the 2012–13 season. The Celtics returned to the playoffs in 2014–15 as a result of that effort, which paid off far sooner than many analysts had anticipated. In that season, the team acquired point guard Isaiah Thomas, who later developed into an All-Star and helped the team to the best record in the Eastern Conference in 2016–17.

After the Celtics were defeated by the Cleveland Cavaliers in four games to one, the team's season came to an end in the conference finals. In the off-season, the Celtics acquired star guard Kyrie Irving through the exchange of Thomas and other assets. Gordon Hayward, an All-Star forward, was also acquired. Despite the fact that both players missed significant amounts of time during the regular season due to injuries, the rest of the young Celtics core performed better than expected, helping Boston to the second-best record in the Eastern Conference and on an unexpectedly long playoff run that resulted in a seven-game conference finals defeat to the Cavaliers. Despite maintaining a largely healthy roster throughout the 2018–19 season, Boston was soundly ousted from the playoffs in the second round.

After a sluggish start, Boston had the best record in the league from early January through the end of the season in 2021–22.

CHAPTER NINE

Top 5 Coaches in Boston Celtics History

In the 67-year existence of the Celtics club, a total of 16 coaches have been employed. However, only six of the 17 banners that have been hoisted to the rafters were included.

In our top five are:

No Five: Bill Russell

Periods: 1967–1969

Best: 162-83

Title years: 1968 and 1969,

There was only one other person Red Auerbach trusted to lead the dynasty he had built when he stepped down as the head coach of the Boston Celtics following the 1966 championship season.

The adjustment for Russell, who took on the role of player-coach and became the first black head coach of a major sport, was not entirely smooth at initially. Russell oversaw the Celtics to a 60-21 overall record in 1967, but his squad's five-game loss to Wilt Chamberlain and the Philadelphia 76ers ended Boston's eight-year title streak.

Russell, though, bounced back the next two seasons in typical fashion. In 1968 and 1969, his teams won a combined 102 games and the championships. At the conclusion of the decade, the Celtics' lineup was getting older, but Russell persisted in guiding them to the pinnacle of basketball.

One of the greatest finals surprises in league history occurred when Russell led Boston to a Game 7 victory over the widely fancied Los Angeles Lakers in his final contest as a Celtic. Russell announced his retirement as a Boston Celtics player and coach soon after the game.

Russell is second in franchise history for postseason winning percentage -619, but only seventh overall for wins due to his short tenure in Boston as a coach - only three seasons.

In the middle of the 1970s, Russell would go on to lead the Seattle Supersonics before making a comeback in 1987 as the leader of the Sacramento Kings. The Celtics legend, though, had little success in those endeavors, making the playoffs in only two of the five seasons combined.

No. Four: Doc Rivers

Periods: 2005–2013

Best: 416-305

Title Years: 2008

When Rivers arrived in Boston, it had been nearly two decades since the Celtics had participated in the NBA Finals. Doc, though, helped hoist the franchise's 17th banner to the storied rafters of the TD Garden after only four seasons with the organization.

For the illustrious club, Rivers is third in both regular season and postseason victories. In his nine seasons as head coach, his team's only twice missed the playoffs while winning six division championships. During their historic postseason run, the

2008 championship squad lost just one game at home while winning the third-most games in franchise history.

But what was most remarkable was how Doc altered Celtic culture. He was given a very mediocre and unlikable group of players in 2004, including an aged Gary Payton, Ricky Davis, and Mark Blount. The team's chemistry was further ruined by a midseason deal that brought Antoine Walker back to Boston, which ultimately resulted in a first-round playoff exit.

All of the abovementioned players left by the spring thaw as Coach Rivers and President of Basketball Operations Danny Ainge worked to restructure the roster. Rivers developed a no hero ball mindset during those years.

Nevertheless, it is challenging to argue that Rivers should rank any higher on this list given his.

In addition, five other Celtics head coaches have led their teams to as many titles as Rivers. It is tough to ignore the fact that Doc managed the second-worst team in the franchise's 67-year history, 24-58, in 2007, and that his 11-16 record in close-out games as coach is hardly impressive.

No Three: K.C. Jones

Periods: 1984–1988

Best: 308-102

Title Years: 1984, 1986

There was a lot of blame to go around when the 1983 Boston Celtics were routed by the Milwaukee Bucks in the conference playoffs, 4-0. Coach Bill Fitch, a harsh enforcer who was not hesitant to openly criticize his players, became a target in the Celtic locker room and eventually quit in the winter.

Lead assistant K.C. Jones took his place, replacing him with a personality that contrasted greatly with Fitch's strict ways: calm, kind demeanour.

Before taking on the role of team head coach, Jones was already a Celtic icon. On Boston's 8 straight championship teams, the coach, who is renowned for his defensive acumen, played an important part. Expectations were quite high when team president Red Auerbach named Jones head coach at the beginning of the 1984 season.

At the beginning of the 1984 season, K.C. realized the quality he had been given, and his ideology evolved into something rather straightforward. I pay attention to the performers. My role is to provide them with guidance and a foundation from which to work, but you must allow them to exercise their own imagination and creativity. They must be permitted to participate because it is their game.

K.C. Jones led the Celtics to four consecutive finals trips between the 1984 and 1987 seasons. Since then, no coach in the league has managed to duplicate this achievement. Only Auerbach had more postseason victories, and his.751 regular-season winning % is the best in the franchise's lengthy history. No Celtic team Jones led won less than 57 games, and the 1986 club is widely regarded as the best in NBA history.

Nevertheless, K.C. Jones's insight went far beyond the win-loss record, as six different members of his roster from 1986 went on to become NBA head coaches.

No Two: Tom Heinsohn

Periods: 1970–1978

Best: 427-263

Title Years: 1974, 1976

When coach Tom Heinsohn came in 1970, the job of resurrecting the Boston Celtic dynasty seemed insurmountable.

The Celtics went into the 1970s with great expectations after claiming nine championships in the previous ten years. Sadly, they didn't have a coach in Cousy, Russell, Jones, or Auerbach when the decade began.

Whatever the case, Tommy Heinsohn contributed to the nearly seamless transition from the Bird age of the 1980s to the dynasty of the 1960s. Heinsohn developed a gritty, hard-nosed, and brisk team that would add to the Celtics' championship history just five years after retiring as a Hall of Fame player and with no prior head coaching experience.

The 1970s championship teams did not have a ton of Hall of Famers, in contrast to the dynasty teams that were led by Heinsohn before and the four championship teams that would come after. On either of Heinsohn's championship-winning teams, only Dave Cowens and John Havlicek were members of the Hall of Fame.

Nevertheless, the six-time All-Star and former Rookie of the Year led Boston to the NBA's top teams.

In each of his first four seasons, Heinsohn raised the team's win total. The 1973 Celtics squad had the best record in franchise history with a 68-14 mark. Heinsohn was only the second coach in the long history of the team to get the honor when the 1973 season came to a close. The next year, he led the Celtics to their first of two championships.

Tom Heinsohn won almost 400 games during his eight seasons as the franchise's head coach, and despite the fact that the Boston teams of the 1970s are all too frequently forgotten in Celtic legend, he won five division titles during that span.

Tom Heinsohn is the only head coach of the Boston Celtics to have more victories than Red Auerbach.

No One: Red Auerbach

Periods: 1951 to 1966.

Best: 795-397

Title years: 1957, '59–66

The Boston Celtics are a philosophy; they are not a basketball team.

Red Auerbach's iconic remarks are still ingrained deeply in the Boston Celtics organization to this day. And if the Celtics are a way of life, then Red Auerbach, the team's coach, deserves a lot of credit for helping those who have benefited.

The Celtics had only been in Boston for four years at the time they arrived at the beginning of the 1951 season, and they had never finished above.500 and had only once made the playoffs. Owner Walter Brown yearned to make an impact, but Auerbach insisted on having his way with things.

The local media and supporters alike were incensed when Auerbach decided not to select local icon Bob Cousy in the 1950 draft. After failing to reach an agreement with the Tri-Cities Blackhawks a few months later, Cousy would sign.

Chuck Cooper, the first black player ever selected in a professional basketball draft, was chosen by Auerbach in the same selection. In addition, 14 years after Cooper was selected by Auerbach's Celtics, they would be the first NBA team to go into a game with an all-black starting lineup.

Red's crowning achievement occurred during the 1956 NBA Draft when he dealt six-time All-Star Ed MaCauley to St. Louis in exchange for Bill Russell, a center out of the University of San Francisco. The basketball scene in Boston would never be the same with Red and Russell together.

No coach in any sport has led as many championship-winning teams in a row as Auerbach, and only Phil Jackson has won more titles than Red's nine. With the Celtics, he has 795 victories, more than 300 more than the next player on the all-time wins list. With the exception of Jerry Sloan and Gregg Popovich, Auerbach led the Celtics to more victories than any other organization.

In terms of games coached, victories, playoff victories, and of course championships for the team, he comes in first. In fact, Auerbach's eight titles are more than all the other Celtic coaches on this list put together.

In each of his eight last seasons, Auerbach won 50 or more games. The fact that Boston never finished below.500 and made the postseason in his 16 seasons as Celtics coach may be of most significance.

Auerbach had an ongoing influence on the Celtics organization even after he retired in 1966. Red was the team's general manager for the remainder of the decade and into the 1980s, and his influence was felt throughout the organization.

Red Auerbach would play a key role in the orchestration of eight more championships in Boston, from selecting Bill Russell to succeed him as head coach to selecting Larry Bird in 1978 and trading for Robert Parish and Kevin McHale.

In 1965, Auerbach was also voted Coach of the Year, an honor that bears his name to this day.

He was chosen to the NBA's Silver Anniversary Team in 1971, and Red Auerbach was voted one of the Top 10 Coaches in NBA History in 1997 as part of the NBA at 50 commemoration.